Jackie Robinson

BASEBALL PIONEER

BY HOWARD REISER

Franklin Watts
New York   London   Toronto   Sydney
A First Book

Cover photograph copyright © : UPI/Bettmann Newsphotos

Photographs copyright © : AP/Wide World Photos: pp. 22, 24, 32, 38, 39, 45, 48 bottom, 52 top, 56; UPI/Bettmann Newsphotos: pp. 11, 16, 18, 26, 29, 35, 42, 44, 47, 48 top, 49, 52 bottom, 55; National Baseball Hall of Fame and Museum, Cooperstown, N.Y.: pp. 28, 54; Culver Pictures, Inc.: p. 26.

Library of Congress Cataloging-in-Publication Data

Reiser, Howard.
    Jackie Robinson : baseball pioneer / Howard Reiser.
       p.   cm. — (A First book)
    Includes bibliographical references and index.
    Summary: A biography of the Hall of Fame baseball player who stood
up to prejudice and threats on his life to prove his ability and
become the first black to play in the major leagues.
    ISBN 0-531-20095-7
    1. Robinson, Jackie, 1919–1972—Juvenile literature.   2. Baseball
players—United States—Biography—Juvenile literature.
[1. Robinson, Jackie, 1919–1972. 2. Baseball players. 3. Afro-
Americans—Biography.] I. Title. II. Series.
GV865.R65R45   1992
796.357'092—dc20
[B]   91-28617 CIP AC

 # CONTENTS

The author would like to thank:
Irving Rudd, Floyd Patterson, William "Pop" Gates,
Duke Snider, Tom Gorman, and Bill Deane of the
Baseball Hall of Fame.

INTRODUCTION

A thirteen-year-old boy dashed home excitedly at the end of the school day. He would soon meet his baseball hero, Jackie Robinson. I know a lot about that meeting. I was that boy.

Nearly forty years have passed since my mother telephoned Jackie Robinson at his off-season office and asked whether I could spend some time with him. She told Robinson he was my favorite baseball player. "My son would love to meet you," my mother said.

Robinson replied without hesitation: "It would be my pleasure to meet your son. Let's set up an appointment."

So on December 2, 1953, my mother and I visited Jackie Robinson in his office in the RCA building in New York City. For more than an hour we spoke about baseball and other topics of interest. Robinson pa-

9

tiently answered each of my many questions, often saying that the questions were very good. He made me feel very proud and happy.

I remember telling Robinson about an older friend of mine. My friend was a great athlete; unfortunately, he had a very bad temper. He often yelled at his own teammates, as well as at *opposing* players. When a teammate made a bad play, my friend would become very upset.

"That is very bad," Robinson said, shaking his head sadly. "A player should not become angry when a teammate does not do well. No one is going to succeed all the time. But he or she should always be encouraged, not made to feel bad. I would hope your friend learns that lesson."

Months later, my friend got angry at a teammate who struck out. He made the teammate feel very sad. Afterwards, I told my friend what Jackie Robinson had said about this type of behavior and he looked at me suspiciously. He did not believe I had spoken to Robinson.

I rose from my chair, left the room, and soon returned with a baseball signed by Robinson. I showed it to my friend. On the ball was inscribed, "To my friend, Howard. Best wishes. Jackie Robinson."

I still have the autographed baseball. I also have a vivid memory of my friend later thanking me for the advice Jackie Robinson had offered. My friend said

Jackie Robinson, pictured here with some of his trophies at
his home in New York, was a generous man. Not many famous
athletes would take the time to meet with a thirteen-year-old
boy simply because the youngster was a fan.

Robinson's guidance had helped teach him a valuable lesson.

Millions of others have also learned valuable lessons from the life of Jackie Robinson.

In the 1800s a handful of blacks played professional baseball. In 1887 an unofficial *color barrier* was imposed in the major leagues. In 1947 Jackie Robinson broke through this color barrier and became the first black major-league player in modern baseball history.

Jackie Robinson overcame racial *prejudice* and threats against his life to become an American hero. Because of him, children of all races can now dream of becoming professional baseball players. Jackie showed that people should be judged for their ability, character, and courage—not for the color of their skin or the *ethnic group* they belong to. This lesson should always be remembered.

1 LEAVING THE SOUTH BEHIND

On the evening of January 31, 1919, the wind swept through the cracks in the walls of an old, run-down cabin outside Cairo, Georgia. Inside the cabin, the fifth child of Jerry and Mallie Robinson had just been born. His name was Jack Roosevelt Robinson.

Jackie Robinson was the grandson of a slave. His father was a *sharecropper*. He worked on someone else's land and was entitled to half of what he grew. The owner received the other half.

Soon after Jackie was born, Jerry Robinson announced that he had grown tired of farm work. He told Mallie he was taking a big trip to look for another job. He never returned.

With her husband gone, Mallie and her children were forced to leave the farm. For a while, they lived elsewhere in Georgia. But conditions in the South were bad for blacks. Black schools and churches were being burned. Black families lived in constant fear for their lives.

One day, Mallie gathered her children around her. "We are taking a long bus ride," she announced. "Your Uncle Burton lives in Pasadena, California. He says it is very nice there. He has invited us to live with him."

It took courage for Mallie to decide to move far from many family members and friends. But she was certain her decision would help her and her children to enjoy happier and better lives than they would experience in the *segregated* South. A religious woman, Mallie had faith she was doing the right thing.

In May of 1920, Mallie packed the family's *meager* belongings inside suitcases and boxes and boarded the bus to California with her five children: Edgar, ten; Frank, nine; Mack, five; Willa Mae, four; and Jackie, who was only sixteen months old.

Upon arriving in California, the Robinsons were greeted by Uncle Burton and his family. The family lived in a crowded three-room apartment that had no hot water. But to Mallie Robinson it was beautiful. She was very happy for the chance to begin a new life with her children.

Soon after moving into Uncle Burton's home, Mallie began working as a laundress. She worked long hours washing and ironing clothes for others. But Mallie Robinson never complained. She had faith that conditions would improve in the future.

And Mallie's faith was soon rewarded. Just two years after arriving in Pasadena, she had saved enough money from her work to move into a new house at 121 Pepper Street. Mallie was very happy. But she soon learned that *racial discrimination* existed in California, just as it existed in Cairo, Georgia.

Neighbors signed *petitions* to force the Robinsons to move. They burned a cross in front of the Robinson house. They cursed the Robinson children. They did everything they could to make the family unhappy. But Mallie was determined to remain in her home.

Jackie never forgot his early experiences facing racial prejudice. As an adult, he often recalled an incident that occurred when he was eight years old.

Jackie was outside his home when a young girl yelled out, "Nigger, nigger!" Jackie yelled back. The girl's father ran from the house cursing Jackie and throwing rocks at him. The incident ended when the man's wife scolded her husband for fighting with an eight-year-old boy.

Thus Jackie understood at a young age that blacks and whites were not treated equally in Pasadena. Blacks could not use the public swimming pool or the neighborhood YMCA more than once a week. Blacks

who went to a movie were made to sit in the balcony. Such unfair practices made Jackie angry. He promised himself that when he got older he would fight against all acts of discrimination.

Despite the racial *bigotry* that existed, Jackie loved growing up at 121 Pepper Street. He and his friends often relaxed together in the house, enjoying its warm, *homey* atmosphere. Jackie was very thankful for the love that existed in his home. "My family was very close," he later recalled. "We had wonderful times together."

While growing up, Jackie would often be alone after a busy day at school because Mallie Robinson worked long hours to support her family. As a result, Jackie sometimes felt lonely. To help keep himself busy, he joined a gang.

The group, known as the Pepper Street Gang, never hurt anyone, but it did get into mischief. Gang members often hid behind bushes at a golf course. When a ball was hit over a hill, Jackie and his friends would retrieve it. After collecting many balls, they

Robinson would fight for equal rights later in his life. Here he stands, second from right, ready to help lead a parade with the Congress on Racial Equality in San Francisco.

Robinson knew what it was like to be a child with
nothing to do and no place to go. As an adult, he
worked with boys at a Harlem YMCA, teaching them
how to play basketball and, of course, baseball.

would return to the golf club and sell the balls to golfers. They would do the same with baseballs hit over the outfield fences.

The gang would also steal fruit from fruit stands and throw it at passing cars. The boys were often given stern warnings by neighborhood police officers. Had it not been for Carl Anderson, a kind shop merchant, Jackie might have gotten into serious trouble.

Anderson warned Jackie that he could be headed for jail if he remained with the gang. He said Mallie Robinson would be heartbroken if her son were ever arrested. "You must quit the gang," Anderson admonished Jackie. "Don't break your mother's heart."

Jackie would never do anything to hurt his mother. He quit the gang the next day.

2 OUTSTANDING ATHLETE

At Muir Technical High School, Jackie starred on the football, basketball, baseball, and track teams. Members of opposing teams often tried to upset him by calling him names, but such actions did not help them win. In fact, they inspired Jackie to do even better.

Jackie's brother Frank attended most of Jackie's events. Frank always encouraged his younger brother. When Jackie was a high school senior, Frank was certain Jackie would win an athletic *scholarship* to college. Frank was very angry when Jackie was not offered any such scholarship.

But Jackie was not discouraged. He enrolled at Pasadena Junior College, the same school that his brother Mack had attended. A year earlier, at the 1936 Olympic Games in Berlin, Germany, Mack had won a silver medal for finishing second in the 2,000-meter run. Jackie was very proud of his brother.

Shortly after entering college, Jackie flashed his own outstanding athletic skills. But first he had to recover from a broken ankle suffered during an early football practice. Upon returning to action, Jackie played *quarterback*. He led PJC to five wins and one tie in the last six games. Later in the year, Jackie was the basketball team's high scorer.

Old-timers recall Jackie's greatest day as a junior college athlete. An important track meet and a championship baseball game were scheduled on the same afternoon, 40 miles (64 km) apart. It did not appear possible that Robinson could compete in both events.

But Jackie was not one to give up easily. He received permission to be the first person to compete in the broad jump, then promptly set a broad jump record of 25 feet 6½ inches (7.79 m). He then sped off to the baseball game in a waiting car.

Robinson was immediately inserted into the lineup after arriving late for the game. He helped Pasadena win the game, and the Southern California Junior College baseball championship. Jackie Robinson was voted the most valuable junior college baseball player in Southern California. When he returned home, he was a tired but proud young man.

In the spring of 1939, Robinson prepared to graduate from Pasadena Junior College. Now, dozens of senior colleges were offering him scholarships to play on their

Although famous for his baseball skills, Robinson was also gifted as a college football, track, and (pictured here) basketball star.

teams. After much thought, Robinson chose the University of California at Los Angeles (UCLA). Frank would still be able to watch his brother play— something he could not do had Jackie decided to attend a school far from home.

But tragedy soon struck. In May, Frank was killed in a motorcycle accident. The Robinson family was heartbroken. Jackie helped ease his deep sorrow by looking forward to entering college in September and doing well in sports. The coaches at UCLA could hardly wait for Robinson's arrival.

Shortly after the football season began, Robinson had already become a campus hero. Because he was very fast and skillful, it was difficult for other teams to tackle him. During one game, Robinson ran 65 yards (59.4 m) for a winning touchdown. In another, he ran more than 80 yards (73.2 m). Unfortunately, Robinson hurt his left ankle with three games left in the season. He played the remaining games in considerable pain.

But Robinson did not rest his injury after the season ended. He immediately joined the basketball team, which had already begun its season. Even though he had gotten off to a late start, he quickly displayed his basketball skills. In twelve games, he was the leading scorer in the league.

With the season over, Robinson set his sights on baseball and track. He played shortstop on the baseball

Talent is not all you need to be a successful athlete;
you also need to work hard. Here, Robinson practices
at UCLA before beginning his outstanding career there.

team. In track, he won many honors in broad jump competitions. At the end of the year, Jackie was the first athlete at UCLA to earn a letter in four sports.

In his second year, Robinson again starred in football and basketball. But he felt bad that his mother still worked hard to support the family. So, when the basketball season ended in 1941, Jackie Robinson announced he was leaving school so he could work full-time. Mallie Robinson was very upset with her son's decision. But he had made up his mind.

Robinson first worked as an athletic director at a camp. He then traveled to Hawaii, where he worked for a construction company on weekdays and played for the Honolulu Bears professional football team on Sundays. However, Robinson did not work long enough to earn much money for his family. On December 7, 1941, the Japanese bombed Pearl Harbor. The United States then declared war on Japan. It wasn't long before Jackie Robinson was *drafted* into the U.S. Army.

Jackie Robinson was assigned to Fort Riley, Kansas, for basic training. After finishing training, Robinson applied to Officer Candidate School. Although he had passed the examinations, he had not received any word about being admitted into the school. Other black soldiers had also not yet been accepted.

Robinson knew that the black soldiers had not

As usual, Robinson won the track-and-field event he competed in at UCLA.

been admitted simply because of their skin color. He complained to heavyweight boxing champion Joe Louis, who was also stationed at Fort Riley. Louis, a black man, was probably the most famous athlete in the world. After grimly listening to Robinson's story, Louis promised to try to help. Soon, Jackie and other blacks were accepted into the school. Shortly there-after, Jackie Robinson rose to the rank of lieutenant.

Robinson was assigned to Fort Hood, Texas. One day, the driver of an Army bus ordered him to move to the rear of the bus. Robinson knew that blacks sat in the rear of buses in the South, but segregation was not permitted in the Army. Robinson refused to change his seat.

The driver reported the incident. When Robinson got off the bus, the military police grabbed him. He was made to appear before Army captain Gerald M. Bear. Then Robinson was ordered to face a military trial. He was charged with not following orders and failing to show respect to a higher-level officer.

It appeared Robinson would be unfairly punished. But when people read about the case in the newspapers, they got angry. Many wrote letters to newspapers and to elected public officials in support of Robinson. The public support helped Jackie beat the charges.

While waiting for his Army release, Robinson con-

(Facing page) Robinson, as a World War II soldier.
While in the Army, Robinson would fight racial discrimination—
something he would continue to do throughout his life.

tacted the Kansas City Monarchs black professional baseball team. The Monarchs told Jackie they wanted him for their club. Robinson joined the Monarchs in April of 1945, several months after his discharge from the Army. He did not realize then that this decision would lead to his making baseball history only six months later.

③ PLAY BALL!

Robinson enjoyed spring training with the Monarchs in Houston, Texas. He was the starting shortstop. He was paid well, and he was expected to be an important player on the team.

But as time passed, Robinson grew unhappy. Bus travel was uncomfortable. The Monarchs players often slept on the bus because many hotels would not accept blacks. The team also had to eat on the bus often because blacks were commonly refused service in restaurants and roadside diners. Each day, Robinson became increasingly bitter at the way he and his teammates were forced to live.

He was also concerned about his future. Robinson understood the importance of obtaining a secure, year-round job. The money earned at work could be used to help support his mother and to marry and support Rachel Isum, a young woman he had met at UCLA.

Robinson, as a
Kansas City Monarch

While Jackie Robinson was considering his options, Brooklyn Dodgers general manager Branch Rickey had begun a search for a black player. Rickey was hoping that the search would lead to his signing a black to play in the major leagues. But he did not tell his scouts of his intentions. They thought they were scouting players for a new team in the black leagues.

Rickey's scouts carefully evaluated every player in the black leagues. They filed extensive reports, including information on each player's background, personal habits, and temperament. Rickey had demanded such information. He knew that a black major leaguer must be a person of intelligence, character, and courage, in addition to having outstanding athletic ability.

Rickey studied every report filed by his scouting staff. A number of players appeared to have the ability for the major leagues. But the reports on one player stood out above the rest. The player's name was Jackie Robinson.

On the morning of August 28, 1945, Brooklyn Dodgers scout Clyde Sukeforth accompanied Robinson to the downtown Brooklyn offices of Branch Rickey. After shaking Robinson's hand, Rickey asked the ballplayer whether he knew the reason for their meeting. Robinson answered that he had heard that a new black team was being formed and that he might be asked to join it.

Rickey told Robinson there would be no such team. He explained that he wanted Robinson to be the first black in modern baseball history to play in the major leagues. Rickey said he wanted Robinson to sign a contract with the Dodgers' organization.

Jackie Robinson could not believe his ears. For a moment, he could barely speak. But that was okay— the Dodgers' boss was doing most of the talking anyway.

Pacing the floor and waving a big cigar, Rickey warned Robinson that he would face a very troublesome time. He said pitchers would throw at his head and runners would try to spike him. He warned that he would be called "nigger" and other ugly names, and would not be able to stay with his team in many hotels and restaurants. It would be even more difficult, Rickey warned, because Robinson would not be allowed to fight back or speak out against injustices.

"Mr. Rickey, do you want a Negro player who is afraid to fight back?" Jackie asked. Rickey roared, "I want a player with the guts enough not to fight back."

Their meeting lasted three hours. At one point, Rickey asked Robinson whether he was certain that he wished to go through with it. Robinson paused briefly. Then, looking Rickey straight in the eye, he answered that he was not afraid to meet the challenge.

On October 23, 1945, Jackie Robinson signed a

Jack Roosevelt Robinson breaks the color barrier in the
major leagues. Branch Rickey, Jr., second from left, watches
as Robinson signs his contract with the Montreal Royals,
the number one farm club of the Brooklyn Dodgers.

contract to play the 1946 season with the Montreal Royals, the Dodgers' top minor-league team. Robinson would soon become the first black to play in a major-league organization. Blacks everywhere rejoiced.

During their meeting, Rickey had encouraged Robinson to marry Rae. Rickey felt that a loving and sincere wife would help Jackie overcome the problems he would face as a black major-league ballplayer. Jackie loved Rae very much. On February 10, 1946, Jackie and Rae were married in a church wedding in California.

Shortly after, Robinson arrived in Florida for spring training with Montreal. The manager, Clay Hopper, was from Mississippi. He had told Rickey he did not want a black on his team. But when Robinson reported, Hopper greeted him warmly.

Jackie Robinson got off to a slow start. He did not play with his usual all-around skill. He hit poorly and did not throw well because of a sore arm. He became discouraged.

But his spirits were lifted by the large numbers of blacks who cheered him on the field and offered encouragement off the field. Many whites also supported

Jackie and Rachel were married before Robinson started spring training in 1946.

37

(Above) On April 18, 1946, Robinson hit a home run in the
third inning to help Montreal beat the Jersey City Giants 14–1.
(Right) Robinson in his Royals' uniform.

him. Toward the end of training, Robinson's performance greatly improved. He began hitting the ball solidly. He was great at second base. And he ran the bases with excitement.

Robinson played outstandingly during the season, despite the immense pressure he faced. Players called him ugly names and pitchers threw at him. Once, a player placed a black cat on the field. "Look at your cousin," the player shouted at Jackie. When Robinson scored a run, he yelled back at the player, "I guess my cousin is happy now."

Jackie Robinson went on to lead the league in hitting, fielding, and runs scored. Montreal then beat Louisville in the Little World Series. Montreal fans carried Jackie around the field in celebration.

By now, Robinson had earned the respect of most baseball people. Even Hopper had grown to admire him. "Jackie's the greatest *competitor* I've ever seen. And he's a gentleman," he told Rickey after the season ended.

④ A PLACE IN HISTORY

Jackie Robinson enjoyed a very happy winter. Rae gave birth to their first child, Jackie Jr. Robinson spent much time with his newborn son during the off-season. He knew it would soon be time to report to Havana, Cuba, where both Montreal and the Dodgers trained.

When spring training began, Robinson hoped he would be promoted to the Dodgers before the start of the season. He helped his chances by playing very well. Even the Dodgers' players were impressed. On April 10, 1947, Rickey issued a press release announcing that Jackie Robinson was now a member of the Dodgers. Robinson's promotion came as the regular season was about to begin.

The signing of Jackie Robinson by the Dodgers angered many people who did not like blacks. Robinson received a lot of hate mail. He was warned that he

In Havana, Cuba, for spring training in early 1947,
Robinson studies a roster of the Brooklyn Dodgers,
probably wondering when his name will appear on it.
He wouldn't have to wait much longer.

and Rae would be shot if he ever played for the Dodgers. Some threatened to kidnap his infant son. Robinson was worried, but he refused to be intimidated. When the season began, Jackie Robinson was the Dodgers' starting first baseman.

A month after the season began, members of the St. Louis Cardinals decided they did not want to play against Robinson. These players tried to persuade members of other teams to do the same. But National League president Ford Frick warned that any player who refused to play would be suspended from baseball. "This is the United States of America," Frick declared. "One citizen has as much right to play as another." The Cardinals players backed down on their threat.

When the Dodgers played in Boston, Braves players and fans shouted names at Jackie. Suddenly, Dodgers shortstop Pee Wee Reese slowly walked toward Jackie. Reese, who came from the South, was one of the most popular players in baseball. Upon reaching his teammate, Pee Wee placed his arm around Jackie's shoulder. The insults stopped at once. Robinson never forgot Pee Wee's act of kindness.

Despite the hardships under which he played, Jackie Robinson had a great season. He batted .297, led the league with 29 stolen bases, and scored 125 runs. He also helped the Dodgers win the National League

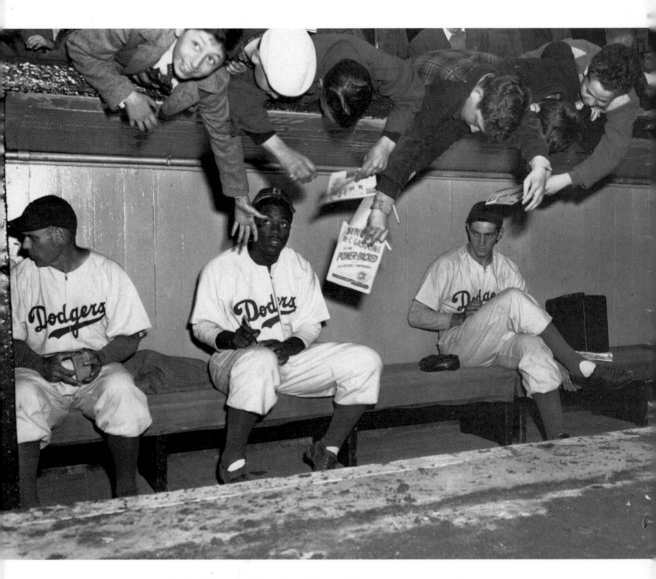

On Robinson's first day with the Dodgers, fans reach over the
Brooklyn dugout at Ebbets Field to try to get his autograph.
(Facing page) Jackie Robinson and Pee Wee Reese.

Pennant, their first in six years. After the Yankees beat the Dodgers in an exciting seven-game World Series, Robinson was voted Rookie of the Year.

During the off-season, Jackie foolishly gained a lot of weight. Because of his poor physical condition, he got off to a slow start in 1948. It was not until the season was well under way that Robinson began to play well. Now the Dodgers' second baseman, he formed a great double-play combination with Reese. The Dodgers, however, disappointed their fans by finishing in third place.

Overall, Jackie had a fine season. He batted .296, one point less than what he hit in his rookie year. More significantly, however, Rickey had already signed four other blacks: pitchers Dan Bankhead, Don Newcombe, and Roy Partlow, and catcher Roy Campanella. Meanwhile, another black, Larry Doby, was playing for the Cleveland Indians in the American League.

In 1949 Robinson was the best player in the National League. He led the league in batting with a .342 average and in stolen bases with 37. He drove in 124 runs, scored 122 times, had 203 hits, and was a great defensive second baseman. On the basepaths, he was the most exciting base runner since Ty Cobb.

Robinson had led the Dodgers to their second pennant in three years. But the Yankees again defeated the Dodgers in the World Series. Jackie's spirits were

Jack Ryan of the Baseball Writers Association presents
Jackie Robinson with the award for "Rookie of the Year"
for 1947. Robinson was selected by a nationwide
poll of sportswriters.

(Facing page) Maybe practicing with his son,
Jackie Jr., is what gave Robinson the skills to
win the National League's Most Valuable Player
award in 1949. At left, Robinson shows
the plaque to his wife and son.
(Above) Robinson steals home in the first
game of the 1955 World Series.

boosted, however, when he was voted the league's Most Valuable Player.

The year was very significant to Jackie in another respect. At the start of the year, he and Rickey agreed that Robinson could now conduct himself as did other players. He could argue with an umpire and fight back against players who tried to hurt him or who yelled insults at him. After three years in the Dodgers organization, a heavy burden was finally removed from Jackie Robinson's shoulders.

Robinson starred with the Dodgers for seven more years, through 1956. He played second base, third base, and left field. During this time, the team won four pennants. Although age and injuries had slowed him down, Robinson was a key player in the 1955 World Series against the New York Yankees. He stole home in the first game. Later, his daring base running and clutch hitting helped the Dodgers to win the championship.

Following the 1956 season, Robinson was traded to the New York Giants. Rickey was no longer the Dodgers boss, having left the club several years earlier to run the Pittsburgh Pirates. Although Robinson would soon be thirty-eight years old, the Giants felt he was still good enough to help them win a pennant. To their deep disappointment, Jackie Robinson never wore a Giants uniform. He retired from baseball.

5 LIFE AFTER BASEBALL

Athletes are often unhappy after they retire from sports. They are no longer cheered in stadiums, written about in newspapers, or discussed on television and radio sportscasts. For many former sports heroes, it is a difficult period of adjustment.

Jackie Robinson did not face any such problem. He and Rae now had two other children—Sharon and David. Robinson could now spend more time with his growing family. He also became involved with many activities.

Robinson became vice president of Chock Full O' Nuts, a restaurant chain. He wrote a newspaper column. He marched in parades and took part in demonstrations to improve conditions for blacks. And he became a high-level assistant to New York governor Nelson Rockefeller, advising the governor on civil rights matters.

Robinson sits with his family at their Stamford, Connecticut, home on January 6, 1957, after he confirmed that he would retire from baseball. The following day he packed up his baseball gear in the Dodgers dressing room at Ebbets Field.

A highlight of Robinson's life occurred when he became the first black to be elected into baseball's Hall of Fame in Cooperstown, New York. Jackie was voted into the Hall in his first year of eligibility, a rare accomplishment. On July 23, 1962, more than 5,000 persons attended the induction ceremonies. Those present included Jackie's mother, his wife, and Branch Rickey.

In his speech, Robinson hailed them as "three of the most wonderful people I know." He also thanked all those who "were so wonderful during those trying days."

Later, Robinson happily signed autographs. He then excitedly snapped pictures of other baseball greats gathered for the occasion, as well as of other activities surrounding the event. Jackie did not want to miss a thing. He was determined to capture every moment of this wonderful day.

Sadly, Robinson suffered greatly in the following years. Jackie Jr. was wounded and became a drug addict in the Vietnam War. After his discharge, he was arrested on drug charges. Jackie Jr. eventually overcame his drug problems and worked hard to help other addicts straighten out their lives. His future appeared bright.

But tragedy struck when Jackie Jr. was killed in a car accident in June of 1971. It was the middle of the night, and he was riding home from an anti-drug program. He was only twenty-four years old.

Branch Rickey, Rachel Robinson, and Mallie Robinson
(Jackie's mother) are with the star when Robinson became
the first black to be inducted into the Baseball Hall of Fame.
(Facing page) Jackie Robinson was highly respected throughout
his life. Here he and the Reverend Martin Luther King, Jr. (right),
receive honorary doctor-of-law degrees from Howard University.

Some of Robinson's ex-teammates carry his casket
from Riverside Church in New York City after his
funeral service on October 27, 1972.

Robinson's own health had been poor for a number of years. He suffered from diabetes and heart problems. The diabetes caused him to lose much of his sight. He often appeared tired and old. On October 24, 1972, more than a year after the death of his son, Jackie suffered a heart attack in his home in Stamford, Connecticut. He was pronounced dead at the age of fifty-three.

More than 2,500 persons attended Jackie Robinson's funeral at Riverside Church in New York City. Thousands more stood outside. With tears streaming down their cheeks, they heard the Reverend Jesse Jackson deliver the *eulogy*.

"Today we must balance the tears of sorrow with tears of joy," Reverend Jackson told the mourners. He said that although Robinson had died, his impact on society would last forever. "When Jackie took the field," he continued, "something reminded us of our birthright to be free."

 # GLOSSARY

Bigotry—behavior showing the prejudice of a person who is not tolerant of other people's race, opinions, and beliefs.

Color barrier—a racist condition that prevents someone from accomplishing something because of his or her skin color.

Competitor—one who participates in various contests or games; a person who wants to win against a rival.

Draft—the summoning of a person by the government to serve in the armed forces.

Ethnic group—people distinguished by customs or language.

Eulogy—a speech or statement in praise of a dead person.

Homey—comfortable, friendly, cozy.

Integrate—to unify; to remove segregation barriers.

Meager—a small amount.

Opposing—to compete against, such as playing against a person or a team.

Petitions—a formal written document requesting a particular action from a person or group in power.

Prejudice—a preconceived hatred or dislike without just cause.

Quarterback—an important position on a football team. The quarterback usually calls the offensive signals, and is the one who passes the ball.

Racial discrimination—the unfair treatment of a person or persons because of their skin color.

Scholarship—a gift of money, or the offering of other assistance, to help a student with school expenses.

Segregate—restricted or separated by group or race.

Sharecropper—a tenant farmer who receives a share of the crop for working farmland owned by someone else.

FOR FURTHER READING

Adler, David. *Jackie Robinson: He Was the First*. New York: Holiday House, 1989.

Alvarez, Mark. *The Official Baseball Hall of Fame Story of Jackie Robinson*. New York: Simon & Schuster, 1990.

Cohen, Barbara. *Thank You, Jackie Robinson*. New York: Lothrop, Lee & Shepard, 1974.

Davidson, Margaret. *The Story of Jackie Robinson, Bravest Man in Baseball*. New York: Dell, 1988.

Greene, Carol. *Jackie Robinson: Baseball's First Black Major Leaguer*. Chicago: Childrens Press, 1990.

Rudeen, Kenneth. *Jackie Robinson*. New York: Crowell, 1971.

 INDEX

Page numbers in *italics* refer to illustrations.

Anderson, Carl, 19

Bankhead, Dan, 46
Baseball Hall of Fame, 53, *54*
Bear, Gerald M., 27
Berlin Olympic Games (1936), 20
Black leagues, 30, 31–33
Brooklyn Dodgers, 33–37, *35*, 41–50, *42*, 44–45

Campanella, Roy, 46
Chock Full O'Nuts, 51
Cleveland Indians, 46
Cobb, Ty, 46
Congress on Racial Equality, *16*

Doby, Larry, 46

Fort Hood, TX, 27
Fort Riley, KS, 25, 27
Frick, Ford, 43

Hall of Fame, 53, *54*
Honolulu Bears, 25
Hopper, Clay, 37, 40

 # ABOUT THE AUTHOR

Howard Reiser spoke with Jackie Robinson many times; the first time was when the author was thirteen years old. Mr. Reiser has been a New York City newspaper reporter, columnist, City Hall bureau chief, and labor news writer/editor. Now a political speechwriter, he is the author of *Skateboarding*, published by Franklin Watts. Reiser and his wife, Adrienne, live in New York. They have four children, Philip, Helene, Steven, and Stuart.